Quick & Easy Microwave Recipes

Tom Braxton

Quick & Easy Microwave Recipes

Copyright © 2023 - All rights reserved.

Table of the Contents

Quick & Easy Microwave Recipes

Quick & Easy Microwave Recipes

Quick & Easy Microwave Recipes

Breakfast and Brunch

Microwave Omelette

Ingredients:

- 2 eggs
- 1 tablespoon milk
- Salt and pepper
- 2 tablespoons shredded cheddar cheese
- Optional toppings: diced tomatoes, diced bell peppers, chopped ham, cooked bacon

Instructions:

1. In a microwave-safe bowl, whisk together the eggs, milk, salt, and pepper.
2. Microwave the mixture on high for 1 minute.
3. Sprinkle the cheese and any desired toppings on one side of the omelette.
4. Fold the other side over the toppings and microwave for an additional 30 seconds or until the cheese is melted.

Microwave Blueberry Muffin

Ingredients:

- 1/4 cup all-purpose flour
- 1/4 teaspoon baking powder
- 1/8 teaspoon salt
- 2 tablespoons granulated sugar
- 2 tablespoons milk
- 1 tablespoon vegetable oil
- 1/4 teaspoon vanilla extract
- 2 tablespoons fresh blueberries

Instructions:

1. In a microwave-safe mug, whisk together the flour, baking powder, salt, and sugar.
2. Stir in the milk, vegetable oil, and vanilla extract until well combined.
3. Gently fold in the blueberries.
4. Microwave on high for 1 minute and 30 seconds, or until the muffin is cooked through.

Microwave Banana Bread Oatmeal

Ingredients:

- 1/2 cup rolled oats
- 1/2 cup milk
- 1/2 cup water
- 1/2 ripe banana, mashed
- 1 tablespoon honey
- 1/2 teaspoon vanilla extract
- 1/4 teaspoon ground cinnamon
- Pinch of salt
- Optional toppings: sliced bananas, chopped nuts, raisins, maple syrup

Instructions:

1. In a microwave-safe bowl, combine the oats, milk, water, mashed banana, honey, vanilla extract, cinnamon, and salt.
2. Microwave on high for 2-3 minutes, stirring halfway through, or until the oatmeal is cooked to your liking.
3. Top with any desired toppings and serve.

Microwave Breakfast Quesadilla

Ingredients:

- 1 small flour tortilla
- 1/4 cup shredded cheddar cheese
- 1 large egg, lightly beaten
- 1 tablespoon milk
- Salt and pepper
- Optional toppings: diced tomatoes, diced bell peppers, sliced avocado, chopped bacon

Instructions:

1. Place the tortilla on a microwave-safe plate and sprinkle the cheese on half of the tortilla.
2. In a small bowl, whisk together the egg, milk, salt, and pepper.
3. Pour the egg mixture over the cheese and any desired toppings.
4. Fold the other half of the tortilla over the egg mixture.
5. Microwave on high for 1 minute or until the cheese is melted and the egg is cooked through.
6. Cut the quesadilla into wedges and serve.

Microwave French Toast

Ingredients:

- 2 slices of bread, preferably slightly stale
- 1 large egg
- 1/4 cup milk
- 1/2 teaspoon vanilla extract
- 1/4 teaspoon ground cinnamon
- Pinch of salt
- Butter, for greasing the microwave-safe dish
- Optional toppings: maple syrup, fresh berries, powdered sugar

Instructions:

1. In a shallow bowl, whisk together the egg, milk, vanilla extract, cinnamon, and salt.
2. Grease a microwave-safe dish with butter.
3. Dip each slice of bread into the egg mixture, making sure to coat both sides well.
4. Place the bread in the prepared dish and microwave on high for 1-2 minutes, flipping the bread halfway through, or until the French toast is cooked through.
5. Serve with any desired toppings.

Microwave Frittata

Ingredients:

- 2 large eggs
- 1 tablespoon milk
- Salt and pepper
- 1/4 cup chopped cooked vegetables (such as bell peppers, onions, or spinach)
- 1 tablespoon shredded cheddar cheese
- Optional toppings: diced tomatoes, chopped herbs, hot sauce

Instructions:

1. In a microwave-safe bowl, whisk together the eggs, milk, salt, and pepper.
2. Stir in the chopped cooked vegetables and shredded cheese.
3. Microwave on high for 1-2 minutes, stirring halfway through, or until the frittata is set and the cheese is melted.
4. Top with any desired toppings and serve.

Microwave Cinnamon Roll in a Mug

Ingredients:

- 1/4 cup all-purpose flour
- 1 tablespoon sugar
- 1/4 teaspoon baking powder
- Pinch of salt
- 2 tablespoons milk
- 1 tablespoon vegetable oil
- 1/4 teaspoon vanilla extract
- 1/2 teaspoon ground cinnamon
- 1 tablespoon cream cheese frosting

Instructions:

1. In a microwave-safe mug, whisk together the flour, sugar, baking powder, and salt.
2. Stir in the milk, vegetable oil, and vanilla extract until well combined.
3. Sprinkle the ground cinnamon on top and swirl it into the batter with a knife.
4. Microwave on high for 1 minute and 30 seconds, or until the cinnamon roll is cooked through.
5. Drizzle the cream cheese frosting on top and serve.

Microwave Breakfast Burrito

Ingredients:

- 1 large flour tortilla
- 2 large eggs
- 1 tablespoon milk
- Salt and pepper
- 1/4 cup shredded cheddar cheese
- 2 tablespoons canned black beans, drained and rinsed
- 1 tablespoon salsa
- Optional toppings: diced tomatoes, sliced avocado, chopped cilantro

Instructions:

1. In a microwave-safe bowl, whisk together the eggs, milk, salt, and pepper.
2. Microwave on high for 1-2 minutes, stirring halfway through, or until the eggs are set.
3. Place the tortilla on a microwave-safe plate and sprinkle the shredded cheese on one half of the tortilla.
4. Spoon the cooked eggs and black beans on top of the cheese.
5. Drizzle the salsa on top and fold the other half of the tortilla over the filling.
6. Microwave on high for 1 minute or until the cheese is melted and the burrito is heated through.
7. Top with any desired toppings and serve.

Microwave Banana Oatmeal

Ingredients:

- 1/2 cup quick oats
- 1/2 cup milk
- 1/2 banana, mashed
- 1 tablespoon honey
- 1/2 teaspoon ground cinnamon
- Pinch of salt

Instructions:

1. In a microwave-safe bowl, combine the oats, milk, mashed banana, honey, cinnamon, and salt.
2. Microwave on high for 1-2 minutes, stirring halfway through, or until the oatmeal is cooked through and the desired consistency is reached.
3. Serve hot and enjoy.

Microwave Egg and Veggie Muffin

Ingredients:

- 2 large eggs
- 2 tablespoons milk
- Salt and pepper
- 1/4 cup chopped mixed vegetables (such as bell peppers, onions, and broccoli)
- 1 tablespoon shredded cheddar cheese

Instructions:

1. In a microwave-safe mug, whisk together the eggs, milk, salt, and pepper.
2. Stir in the chopped mixed vegetables and shredded cheddar cheese.
3. Microwave on high for 1-2 minutes, stirring halfway through, or until the egg is set and the cheese is melted.
4. Let cool for a minute or two, then remove the egg muffin from the mug and serve.

Microwave Blueberry Lemon Muffin

Ingredients:

- 1/4 cup all-purpose flour
- 2 tablespoons sugar
- 1/4 teaspoon baking powder
- Pinch of salt
- 1/4 cup fresh blueberries
- 1 tablespoon vegetable oil
- 1 tablespoon milk
- 1/4 teaspoon vanilla extract
- 1/2 teaspoon lemon zest

Instructions:

1. In a microwave-safe mug, whisk together the flour, sugar, baking powder, and salt.
2. Add the fresh blueberries to the dry ingredients and toss to coat.
3. In a small bowl, whisk together the vegetable oil, milk, vanilla extract, and lemon zest.
4. Pour the wet ingredients into the mug with the dry ingredients and mix until well combined.
5. Microwave on high for 1 minute and 30 seconds, or until the muffin is cooked through.
6. Let cool for a minute or two before serving.

Microwave Breakfast Pizza

Ingredients:

- 1 English muffin, split
- 2 tablespoons pizza sauce
- 1/4 cup shredded mozzarella cheese
- 1 large egg
- Salt and pepper
- Optional toppings: sliced mushrooms, chopped cooked bacon, diced tomatoes

Instructions:

1. Place the English muffin halves on a microwave-safe plate and spread the pizza sauce on top of each half.
2. Sprinkle the shredded mozzarella cheese on top of the sauce.
3. Crack the egg into a small microwave-safe bowl and whisk with a fork.
4. Pour the egg over the cheese and toppings.
5. Microwave on high for 1-2 minutes, or until the egg is set and the cheese is melted.
6. Top with any desired toppings and serve hot.

Microwave Breakfast Quesadilla II

Ingredients:

- 1 large egg
- Salt and pepper
- 1 small flour tortilla
- 1/4 cup shredded cheddar cheese
- 1 tablespoon chopped fresh cilantro
- Salsa, for serving

Instructions:

1. In a microwave-safe bowl, whisk together the egg, salt, and pepper.
2. Microwave on high for 1 minute, or until the egg is set.
3. Place the flour tortilla on a microwave-safe plate.
4. Sprinkle the shredded cheddar cheese and chopped cilantro over one half of the tortilla.
5. Fold the other half of the tortilla over the cheese and egg mixture.
6. Microwave on high for 30 seconds to 1 minute, or until the cheese is melted and the tortilla is crispy.
7. Cut into wedges and serve with salsa.

Microwave Omelette in a Mug

Ingredients:

- 2 large eggs
- 1 tablespoon milk
- Salt and pepper
- 1/4 cup shredded cheddar cheese
- Optional fillings: diced ham, chopped spinach, sliced mushrooms, diced bell peppers, chopped onions

Instructions:

1. In a microwave-safe mug, whisk together the eggs, milk, salt, and pepper.
2. Stir in the shredded cheddar cheese and any desired fillings.
3. Microwave on high for 1-2 minutes, stirring every 30 seconds, or until the omelette is cooked through.
4. Let cool for a minute or two before serving.

Microwave Breakfast Burrito II

Ingredients:

- 1 small flour tortilla
- 1 large egg
- Salt and pepper
- 1/4 cup canned black beans, drained and rinsed
- 2 tablespoons salsa
- 2 tablespoons shredded cheddar cheese
- Optional toppings: sliced avocado, chopped cilantro, hot sauce

Instructions:

1. Place the flour tortilla on a microwave-safe plate and microwave on high for 10-15 seconds to warm it up.
2. In a microwave-safe bowl, whisk together the egg, salt, and pepper.
3. Microwave on high for 1 minute, stirring every 20-30 seconds, or until the egg is set.
4. Place the cooked egg, black beans, salsa, and shredded cheddar cheese on top of the flour tortilla.
5. Fold the bottom and sides of the tortilla over the filling, and then roll it up tightly.
6. Microwave on high for 30 seconds to 1 minute, or until the burrito is heated through.

7. Top with any desired toppings and serve hot.

Microwave Huevos Rancheros

Ingredients:

- 1 small corn tortilla
- 1 large egg
- Salt and pepper
- 2 tablespoons canned black beans, drained and rinsed
- 2 tablespoons salsa
- 1 tablespoon shredded cheddar cheese
- Optional toppings: sliced avocado, chopped cilantro, hot sauce

Instructions:

1. Place the corn tortilla on a microwave-safe plate and microwave on high for 10-15 seconds to warm it up.
2. In a microwave-safe bowl, whisk together the egg, salt, and pepper.
3. Microwave on high for 1 minute, stirring every 20-30 seconds, or until the egg is set.
4. Place the cooked egg, black beans, salsa, and shredded cheddar cheese on top of the corn tortilla.

5. Microwave on high for 30 seconds to 1 minute, or until the cheese is melted and the tortilla is crispy.
6. Top with any desired toppings and serve hot.

Microwave Cinnamon Roll Mug Cake

Ingredients:

- 1/4 cup all-purpose flour
- 1/4 teaspoon baking powder
- 1/4 teaspoon cinnamon
- Pinch of salt
- 1/4 cup milk
- 1 tablespoon vegetable oil
- 1 tablespoon brown sugar
- 1/4 teaspoon vanilla extract
- Optional topping: cream cheese frosting

Instructions:

1. In a microwave-safe mug, whisk together the flour, baking powder, cinnamon, and salt.
2. Add the milk, vegetable oil, brown sugar, and vanilla extract to the mug, and stir until well combined.

3. Microwave on high for 1 minute and 30 seconds, or until the cake is cooked through and a toothpick inserted in the center comes out clean.
4. Let cool for a minute or two before adding any desired toppings.

Microwave Breakfast Pizza

Ingredients:

- 1 small flour tortilla
- 1 large egg
- Salt and pepper
- 2 tablespoons pizza sauce
- 2 tablespoons shredded mozzarella cheese
- Optional toppings: cooked bacon, chopped ham, sliced mushrooms, diced bell peppers, sliced onions

Instructions:

1. Place the flour tortilla on a microwave-safe plate and microwave on high for 10-15 seconds to warm it up.
2. In a microwave-safe bowl, whisk together the egg, salt, and pepper.

3. Microwave on high for 1 minute, stirring every 20-30 seconds, or until the egg is set.
4. Spread the pizza sauce over the flour tortilla, leaving a small border around the edge.
5. Top with the cooked egg, shredded mozzarella cheese, and any desired toppings.
6. Microwave on high for 30 seconds to 1 minute, or until the cheese is melted and bubbly.
7. Let cool for a minute or two before slicing and serving.

Microwave Banana Oatmeal

Ingredients:

- 1 ripe banana, mashed
- 1/2 cup rolled oats
- 1/2 cup milk
- 1/2 teaspoon ground cinnamon
- 1/4 teaspoon vanilla extract
- Optional toppings: sliced banana, chopped nuts, honey, maple syrup

Instructions:

1. In a microwave-safe bowl, combine the mashed banana, rolled oats, milk, cinnamon, and vanilla extract.

2. Microwave on high for 2-3 minutes, stirring every minute, or until the oatmeal is cooked through and creamy.
3. Let cool for a minute or two before adding any desired toppings.

Microwave Blueberry French Toast

Ingredients:

- 2 slices bread, cubed
- 1/4 cup fresh or frozen blueberries
- 1/2 cup milk
- 2 large eggs
- 1 tablespoon maple syrup
- 1/2 teaspoon ground cinnamon
- 1/4 teaspoon vanilla extract
- Optional topping: powdered sugar

Instructions:

1. Grease a microwave-safe mug or ramekin.
2. Place the bread cubes and blueberries in the mug or ramekin.

3. In a separate bowl, whisk together the milk, eggs, maple syrup, cinnamon, and vanilla extract.
4. Pour the mixture over the bread and blueberries in the mug or ramekin.
5. Microwave on high for 2-3 minutes, or until the French toast is cooked through and set.
6. Let cool for a minute or two before dusting with powdered sugar and serving.

Microwave Apple Cinnamon Muffin

Ingredients:

- 1/4 cup all-purpose flour
- 1/4 cup quick-cooking oats
- 1 tablespoon brown sugar
- 1/4 teaspoon baking powder
- 1/4 teaspoon ground cinnamon
- Pinch of salt
- 1/4 cup unsweetened applesauce
- 1 tablespoon milk
- 1 tablespoon vegetable oil
- 1/4 teaspoon vanilla extract
- Optional topping: powdered sugar

Instructions:

1. In a microwave-safe mug, whisk together the flour, oats, brown sugar, baking powder, cinnamon, and salt.
2. Add the applesauce, milk, vegetable oil, and vanilla extract, and stir until well combined.
3. Microwave on high for 1 minute and 30 seconds, or until the muffin is cooked through and set.
4. Let cool for a minute or two before dusting with powdered sugar and serving.

Microwave Breakfast Quiche

Ingredients:

- 1 large egg
- 2 tablespoons milk
- Salt and pepper, to taste
- 1/4 cup shredded cheddar cheese
- 2 tablespoons diced ham
- 1 tablespoon chopped scallions
- 1 small microwave-safe bowl or ramekin

Instructions:

1. In a microwave-safe bowl or ramekin, whisk together the egg, milk, salt, and pepper.
2. Add the shredded cheddar cheese, diced ham, and chopped scallions, and stir until well combined.
3. Microwave on high for 1 minute and 30 seconds, or until the quiche is cooked through and set.
4. Let cool for a minute or two before serving.

Microwave Blueberry French Toast

Ingredients:

- 2 slices of bread, cubed
- 1/4 cup fresh blueberries
- 1 large egg
- 2 tablespoons milk
- 1 tablespoon maple syrup
- 1/4 teaspoon vanilla extract
- Optional toppings: powdered sugar, whipped cream

Instructions:

1. In a microwave-safe mug or bowl, layer the bread cubes and fresh blueberries.
2. In a separate bowl, whisk together the egg, milk, maple syrup, and vanilla extract.
3. Pour the egg mixture over the bread and blueberries, making sure everything is coated.
4. Microwave on high for 1 minute and 30 seconds, or until the French toast is cooked through and set.
5. Let cool for a minute or two before adding any desired toppings.

Microwave Cinnamon Roll Mug Cake

Ingredients:

- 1/4 cup all-purpose flour
- 2 tablespoons granulated sugar
- 1/4 teaspoon baking powder
- 1/4 teaspoon ground cinnamon
- Pinch of salt
- 2 tablespoons milk
- 1 tablespoon vegetable oil
- 1/4 teaspoon vanilla extract

- 1 tablespoon cream cheese frosting (store-bought or homemade)

Instructions:

1. In a microwave-safe mug, whisk together the flour, sugar, baking powder, cinnamon, and salt.
2. Add the milk, vegetable oil, and vanilla extract, and stir until smooth.
3. Microwave on high for 1 minute and 15 seconds, or until the cake is cooked through.
4. Let cool for a minute or two, then top with the cream cheese frosting.
5. Serve warm.

Soups and Stews

Microwave Chicken Noodle Soup

Ingredients:

- 1 cup chicken broth
- 1/2 cup diced cooked chicken
- 1/2 cup diced carrots
- 1/2 cup chopped celery
- 1/2 cup egg noodles
- 1/2 teaspoon dried thyme
- Salt and pepper, to taste

Instructions:

1. In a microwave-safe bowl, combine the chicken broth, diced chicken, carrots, and celery.
2. Microwave on high for 3 to 4 minutes, or until the vegetables are tender.
3. Add the egg noodles and dried thyme to the bowl.
4. Microwave on high for an additional 3 to 4 minutes, or until the noodles are cooked through.
5. Season with salt and pepper, to taste.
6. Serve hot.

Microwave Beef Stew

Ingredients:

- 1 pound stew beef, cut into 1-inch pieces
- 1 cup beef broth
- 1/2 cup chopped onion
- 1/2 cup chopped carrots
- 1/2 cup chopped celery
- 1 cup diced potatoes
- 1/2 teaspoon dried thyme
- Salt and pepper, to taste

Instructions:

1. In a microwave-safe bowl, combine the stew beef, beef broth, onion, carrots, celery, and potatoes.
2. Microwave on high for 10 to 12 minutes, or until the beef is cooked through and the vegetables are tender.
3. Stir in the dried thyme and season with salt and pepper, to taste.
4. Microwave on high for an additional 2 to 3 minutes, or until the stew is heated through.
5. Serve hot.

Microwave Tomato Soup

Ingredients:

- 1 can (14 oz) diced tomatoes
- 1/2 cup vegetable or chicken broth
- 1/2 cup milk
- 1/4 cup chopped onion
- 1/4 cup chopped celery
- 1 tablespoon butter
- 1/2 teaspoon dried basil
- Salt and pepper, to taste

Instructions:

1. In a microwave-safe bowl, combine the diced tomatoes, broth, onion, and celery.
2. Microwave on high for 3 to 4 minutes, or until the vegetables are tender.
3. Add the milk, butter, dried basil, salt, and pepper to the bowl.
4. Microwave on high for an additional 1 to 2 minutes, or until the soup is heated through.
5. Blend the soup with an immersion blender or transfer to a blender to puree until smooth.
6. Serve hot.

Microwave Lentil Stew

Ingredients:

- 1 cup lentils, rinsed and drained
- 1 can (14 oz) diced tomatoes
- 1/2 cup vegetable or chicken broth
- 1/2 cup chopped onion
- 1/2 cup chopped carrots
- 1/2 cup chopped celery
- 1 teaspoon minced garlic
- 1/2 teaspoon cumin
- Salt and pepper, to taste

Instructions:

1. In a microwave-safe bowl, combine the lentils, diced tomatoes, broth, onion, carrots, celery, garlic, and cumin.
2. Microwave on high for 15 to 20 minutes, or until the lentils are tender and the vegetables are cooked through.
3. Stir the stew occasionally and add more broth if needed.
4. Season with salt and pepper, to taste.
5. Serve hot.

Microwave Butternut Squash Soup

Ingredients:

- 1 small butternut squash, peeled, seeded, and chopped
- 1/2 cup chopped onion
- 1/2 cup chopped carrot
- 1/2 cup chopped celery
- 2 cloves garlic, minced
- 2 cups vegetable or chicken broth
- 1/4 cup heavy cream
- Salt and pepper, to taste
- 1 tablespoon olive oil

Instructions:

1. In a microwave-safe bowl, combine the butternut squash, onion, carrot, celery, garlic, and olive oil.
2. Microwave on high for 8 to 10 minutes, or until the vegetables are tender.
3. Add the broth to the bowl and microwave on high for an additional 5 minutes.
4. Blend the soup with an immersion blender or transfer to a blender to puree until smooth.
5. Add the heavy cream to the soup and microwave on high for 1 to 2 minutes, or until heated through.
6. Season with salt and pepper, to taste.

Microwave Lentil Soup

Ingredients:

- 1 cup dried lentils, rinsed and drained
- 1/2 cup chopped onion
- 1/2 cup chopped carrots
- 1/2 cup chopped celery
- 2 cloves garlic, minced
- 2 cups vegetable or chicken broth
- 1/2 teaspoon ground cumin
- 1/4 teaspoon ground coriander
- Salt and pepper, to taste

Instructions:

1. In a microwave-safe bowl, combine the lentils, onion, carrots, celery, and garlic.
2. Add the vegetable or chicken broth to the bowl.
3. Microwave on high for 15 to 20 minutes, or until the lentils are tender.
4. Stir in the cumin and coriander.
5. Season with salt and pepper, to taste.
6. Serve hot.

Microwave Minestrone Soup

Ingredients:

- 1/2 cup chopped onion
- 1/2 cup chopped carrots
- 1/2 cup chopped celery
- 1 garlic clove, minced
- 1 can (14.5 oz) diced tomatoes, undrained
- 1 can (15 oz) white beans, drained and rinsed
- 2 cups chicken or vegetable broth
- 1 teaspoon dried oregano
- 1/2 teaspoon dried basil
- Salt and pepper, to taste
- 1/2 cup small pasta shells
- 1/2 cup chopped fresh spinach

Instructions:

1. In a microwave-safe bowl, combine the onion, carrots, celery, and garlic.
2. Microwave on high for 5 to 7 minutes, or until the vegetables are tender.
3. Stir in the diced tomatoes, white beans, chicken or vegetable broth, oregano, basil, salt, and pepper.
4. Microwave on high for 10 to 12 minutes, or until the soup is heated through.

5. Add the pasta shells and microwave on high for an additional 6 to 8 minutes, or until the pasta is tender.
6. Stir in the chopped spinach and let it sit for 1 to 2 minutes until the spinach is wilted.
7. Serve hot.

Microwave Beef and Barley Stew

Ingredients:

- 1 pound beef stew meat
- 1/2 cup chopped onion
- 1/2 cup chopped carrots
- 1/2 cup chopped celery
- 1 garlic clove, minced
- 1/2 cup pearl barley
- 2 cups beef broth
- 1 teaspoon dried thyme
- Salt and pepper, to taste

Instructions:

1. In a microwave-safe bowl, combine the beef stew meat, onion, carrots, celery, and garlic.

2. Microwave on high for 5 to 7 minutes, or until the beef is browned.
3. Add the pearl barley, beef broth, thyme, salt, and pepper to the bowl.
4. Microwave on high for 15 to 20 minutes, or until the beef and barley are tender.
5. Serve hot.

Microwaved Lentil Soup

Ingredients:

- 1 cup dry lentils, rinsed and drained
- 4 cups vegetable broth
- 1 small onion, diced
- 2 garlic cloves, minced
- 1 carrot, peeled and diced
- 1 celery stalk, diced
- 1 bay leaf
- Salt and pepper, to taste
- 2 tablespoons olive oil
- Fresh parsley, chopped, for garnish

Instructions:

1. In a large microwave-safe bowl, add the lentils, vegetable broth, onion, garlic, carrot, celery, bay leaf, salt, and pepper. Stir to combine.
2. Drizzle the olive oil over the lentil mixture and stir to coat.
3. Cover the bowl with a microwave-safe lid or plate and microwave on high for 15 minutes.
4. Stir the soup, remove the bay leaf, and taste for seasoning. Adjust if needed.
5. Serve the lentil soup hot, garnished with chopped parsley.

Microwaved Chicken Noodle Soup

Ingredients:

- 2 cups chicken broth
- 1 boneless, skinless chicken breast, cut into small pieces
- 1 small onion, diced
- 1 celery stalk, diced
- 1 carrot, peeled and diced
- 1 garlic clove, minced
- 1/2 teaspoon dried thyme

- Salt and pepper, to taste
- 1 cup egg noodles
- Fresh parsley, chopped, for garnish

Instructions:

1. In a large microwave-safe bowl, combine the chicken broth, chicken pieces, onion, celery, carrot, garlic, thyme, salt, and pepper.
2. Cover the bowl with a microwave-safe lid or plate and microwave on high for 10 minutes.
3. Stir in the egg noodles and microwave for an additional 5 minutes.
4. Stir the soup and taste for seasoning. Adjust if needed.
5. Serve the chicken noodle soup hot, garnished with chopped parsley.

Microwave Minestrone Soup II

Ingredients:

- 1 can diced tomatoes
- 1/4 cup chopped onion
- 1/4 cup chopped celery
- 1/4 cup chopped carrots
- 1/4 cup frozen peas

- 1/4 cup frozen corn
- 1/4 cup canned kidney beans, drained and rinsed
- 1/4 teaspoon dried basil
- 1/4 teaspoon dried oregano
- 1/4 teaspoon garlic powder
- 2 cups vegetable broth
- Salt and pepper to taste

Instructions:

1. Combine all ingredients in a large microwave-safe bowl and stir well.
2. Cover with a microwave-safe lid or plastic wrap and microwave on high for 8-10 minutes or until the vegetables are tender.
3. Serve hot.

Microwave Potato Soup

Ingredients:

- 2 medium potatoes, peeled and cubed
- 1/2 cup chopped onion
- 2 cloves garlic, minced
- 1 teaspoon dried thyme
- 2 cups chicken broth

- 1/4 cup heavy cream
- Salt and pepper to taste
- Shredded cheddar cheese and chopped chives for topping (optional)

Instructions:

1. In a microwave-safe bowl, combine the potatoes, onion, garlic, thyme, and chicken broth.
2. Microwave on high for 10-12 minutes, or until the potatoes are tender.
3. Use an immersion blender to puree the soup until smooth.
4. Stir in the heavy cream and season with salt and pepper to taste.
5. Microwave for an additional 2-3 minutes, or until heated through.
6. Top with shredded cheddar cheese and chopped chives, if desired.

Creamy Broccoli Cheddar Soup

Ingredients:

- 1 small onion, chopped
- 2 cups chopped broccoli florets

- 1/2 teaspoon garlic powder
- 1/2 teaspoon salt
- 1/4 teaspoon black pepper
- 2 cups chicken or vegetable broth
- 1/2 cup milk
- 1/2 cup shredded cheddar cheese

Instructions:

1. In a microwave-safe bowl, combine the chopped onion, broccoli florets, garlic powder, salt, and black pepper.
2. Pour in the chicken or vegetable broth and stir to combine.
3. Cover the bowl with a microwave-safe lid or plastic wrap, leaving a small vent for steam to escape.
4. Microwave on high for 10-12 minutes, or until the broccoli is tender.
5. Carefully remove the bowl from the microwave and use an immersion blender to puree the soup until smooth.
6. Add the milk and shredded cheddar cheese, stirring until the cheese is melted and the soup is creamy.
7. Microwave for an additional 1-2 minutes to heat through, if necessary. Serve hot.

Beef and Vegetable Stew

Ingredients:

- 1 pound beef stew meat, cut into small pieces
- 1 small onion, chopped
- 2 cups chopped mixed vegetables (such as carrots, potatoes, and celery)
- 1 teaspoon garlic powder
- 1 teaspoon dried thyme
- 1/2 teaspoon salt
- 1/4 teaspoon black pepper
- 2 cups beef broth

Instructions:

1. In a microwave-safe bowl, combine the beef stew meat, chopped onion, mixed vegetables, garlic powder, dried thyme, salt, and black pepper.
2. Pour in the beef broth and stir to combine.
3. Cover the bowl with a microwave-safe lid or plastic wrap, leaving a small vent for steam to escape.
4. Microwave on high for 15-20 minutes, or until the beef is cooked through and the vegetables are tender.
5. Carefully remove the bowl from the microwave and stir the stew to combine. Serve hot.

Microwave Tomato Soup II

Ingredients:

- 1 can of diced tomatoes
- 1 cup of vegetable broth
- 1/2 cup of milk
- 1 tablespoon of butter
- 1/4 teaspoon of garlic powder
- 1/4 teaspoon of onion powder
- salt and pepper to taste

Instructions:

1. In a microwave-safe bowl, mix the diced tomatoes, vegetable broth, garlic powder, onion powder, salt, and pepper.
2. Microwave for 3-4 minutes until heated through.
3. Add the butter and milk, and microwave for an additional 2 minutes.
4. Use an immersion blender or transfer the mixture to a blender and puree until smooth.
5. Serve hot with a garnish of croutons or fresh herbs, if desired.

Microwave Clam Chowder

Ingredients:

- 1 can of clams
- 1 cup of milk
- 1/2 cup of chicken broth
- 1/4 cup of diced onion
- 1/4 cup of diced celery
- 1 tablespoon of butter
- 1 tablespoon of all-purpose flour
- salt and pepper to taste

Instructions:

1. In a microwave-safe bowl, mix the clams (with juice), milk, chicken broth, onion, celery, salt, and pepper.
2. Microwave for 3-4 minutes until heated through.
3. In a separate microwave-safe bowl, melt the butter for 30 seconds.
4. Add the flour to the melted butter and whisk until smooth.
5. Microwave for 1 minute.
6. Add the butter-flour mixture to the soup and microwave for an additional 2-3 minutes until thickened.
7. Serve hot with crackers or crusty bread.

Creamy Tomato Soup

Ingredients:

- 1 can (14.5 oz) diced tomatoes
- 1 cup chicken or vegetable broth
- 1/4 cup heavy cream
- 1 tbsp tomato paste
- 1/4 tsp garlic powder
- 1/4 tsp dried basil
- Salt and pepper, to taste

Instructions:

1. Combine the diced tomatoes, chicken or vegetable broth, tomato paste, garlic powder, and dried basil in a microwave-safe bowl.
2. Microwave on high for 5-6 minutes, until the soup is hot and bubbly.
3. Remove the bowl from the microwave and stir in the heavy cream. Season with salt and pepper to taste.
4. Return the bowl to the microwave and heat for an additional 1-2 minutes, until the soup is heated through and the cream is fully incorporated. Serve hot.

Beef and Vegetable Stew

Ingredients:

- 1 lb beef stew meat
- 1 cup beef broth
- 1 cup diced potatoes
- 1 cup chopped carrots
- 1/2 cup chopped celery
- 1/2 cup chopped onion
- 1/2 tsp garlic powder
- 1/2 tsp dried thyme
- Salt and pepper, to taste

Instructions:

1. Combine the beef stew meat, beef broth, diced potatoes, chopped carrots, chopped celery, chopped onion, garlic powder, and dried thyme in a microwave-safe bowl.
2. Cover the bowl with a microwave-safe lid or plastic wrap and microwave on high for 8-10 minutes, until the vegetables are tender and the beef is cooked through.
3. Remove the bowl from the microwave and season with salt and pepper to taste. Serve hot.

Vegetables and Side Dishes

Microwaved Parmesan Broccoli

Ingredients:

- 1 head of broccoli, cut into florets
- 1 tablespoon olive oil
- 1/4 teaspoon salt
- 1/4 teaspoon black pepper
- 1/4 cup grated Parmesan cheese

Instructions:

1. In a microwave-safe dish, add the broccoli florets and sprinkle with olive oil, salt, and black pepper. Toss to coat.
2. Cover the dish with a microwave-safe lid or plastic wrap, leaving a small vent for steam to escape.
3. Microwave on high for 3-4 minutes, or until the broccoli is tender but still crisp.
4. Remove from the microwave and sprinkle the Parmesan cheese over the broccoli. Toss to coat and serve.

Microwaved Garlic Butter Sweet Potatoes

Ingredients:

- 2 medium sweet potatoes, peeled and cubed
- 2 tablespoons unsalted butter
- 2 garlic cloves, minced
- 1/4 teaspoon salt
- 1/4 teaspoon black pepper
- 1/4 teaspoon smoked paprika

Instructions:

1. In a microwave-safe dish, add the sweet potatoes and sprinkle with salt, black pepper, and smoked paprika. Toss to coat.
2. In a small microwave-safe dish, melt the butter and stir in the minced garlic.
3. Pour the garlic butter over the sweet potatoes and toss to coat.
4. Cover the dish with a microwave-safe lid or plastic wrap, leaving a small vent for steam to escape.
5. Microwave on high for 5-6 minutes, or until the sweet potatoes are tender.
6. Remove from the microwave and serve hot.

Microwaved Spicy Green Beans

Ingredients:

- 1 pound green beans, trimmed
- 1 tablespoon olive oil
- 1/2 teaspoon smoked paprika
- 1/4 teaspoon cayenne pepper
- 1/4 teaspoon garlic powder
- 1/4 teaspoon salt

Instructions:

1. In a microwave-safe dish, add the green beans and sprinkle with olive oil, smoked paprika, cayenne pepper, garlic powder, and salt. Toss to coat.
2. Cover the dish with a microwave-safe lid or plastic wrap, leaving a small vent for steam to escape.
3. Microwave on high for 4-5 minutes, or until the green beans are tender but still crisp.
4. Remove from the microwave and serve hot.

Microwaved Maple Glazed Carrots

Ingredients:

- 1 pound carrots, peeled and sliced into rounds
- 2 tablespoons unsalted butter
- 2 tablespoons maple syrup
- 1/4 teaspoon cinnamon
- 1/4 teaspoon salt
- 1/4 cup chopped pecans (optional)

Instructions:

1. In a microwave-safe dish, add the carrots and sprinkle with salt. Toss to coat.
2. In a small microwave-safe dish, melt the butter and stir in the maple syrup and cinnamon.
3. Pour the maple glaze over the carrots and toss to coat.
4. Cover the dish with a microwave-safe lid or plastic wrap, leaving a small vent for steam to escape.
5. Microwave on high for 5-6 minutes, or until the carrots are tender.
6. Remove from the microwave and sprinkle with chopped pecans, if desired. Serve hot.

Microwaved Lemon Asparagus

Ingredients:

- 1 pound asparagus, trimmed
- 2 tablespoons unsalted butter
- 1 tablespoon freshly squeezed lemon juice
- 1 teaspoon lemon zest
- 1/4 teaspoon salt
- 1/4 teaspoon black pepper

Instructions:

1. In a microwave-safe dish, add the asparagus and sprinkle with salt and black pepper. Toss to coat.
2. In a small microwave-safe dish, melt the butter and stir in the lemon juice and zest.
3. Pour the lemon butter mixture over the asparagus and toss to coat.
4. Cover the dish with a microwave-safe lid or plastic wrap, leaving a small vent for steam to escape.
5. Microwave on high for 3-4 minutes, or until the asparagus is tender but still crisp.
6. Remove from the microwave and serve hot.

Microwaved Balsamic Glazed Brussels Sprouts

Ingredients:

- 1 pound Brussels sprouts, trimmed and halved
- 2 tablespoons olive oil
- 2 tablespoons balsamic vinegar
- 1 tablespoon honey
- 1/4 teaspoon garlic powder
- 1/4 teaspoon salt
- 1/4 teaspoon black pepper

Instructions:

1. In a microwave-safe dish, add the Brussels sprouts and sprinkle with olive oil, garlic powder, salt, and black pepper. Toss to coat.
2. In a small microwave-safe dish, whisk together the balsamic vinegar and honey.
3. Pour the balsamic glaze over the Brussels sprouts and toss to coat.
4. Cover the dish with a microwave-safe lid or plastic wrap, leaving a small vent for steam to escape.
5. Microwave on high for 5-6 minutes, or until the Brussels sprouts are tender.
6. Remove from the microwave and serve hot.

Microwaved Garlic and Herb Potatoes

Ingredients:

- 1 pound baby potatoes, halved
- 2 tablespoons olive oil
- 2 cloves garlic, minced
- 1 teaspoon dried thyme
- 1/2 teaspoon dried rosemary
- 1/4 teaspoon salt
- 1/4 teaspoon black pepper

Instructions:

1. In a microwave-safe dish, add the potatoes and sprinkle with olive oil, minced garlic, dried thyme, dried rosemary, salt, and black pepper. Toss to coat.
2. Cover the dish with a microwave-safe lid or plastic wrap, leaving a small vent for steam to escape.
3. Microwave on high for 8-10 minutes, or until the potatoes are tender.
4. Remove from the microwave and let cool for a few minutes before serving.

Microwaved Sesame Ginger Broccoli

Ingredients:

- 1 pound broccoli florets
- 1 tablespoon sesame oil
- 1 tablespoon soy sauce
- 1 tablespoon honey
- 1 teaspoon grated ginger
- 1/4 teaspoon garlic powder
- 1/4 teaspoon salt
- 1/4 teaspoon black pepper
- 1 tablespoon sesame seeds

Instructions:

1. In a microwave-safe dish, add the broccoli florets and sprinkle with sesame oil, soy sauce, honey, grated ginger, garlic powder, salt, and black pepper. Toss to coat.
2. Cover the dish with a microwave-safe lid or plastic wrap, leaving a small vent for steam to escape.
3. Microwave on high for 4-5 minutes, or until the broccoli is tender but still crisp.
4. Remove from the microwave and sprinkle with sesame seeds before serving.

Microwaved Sweet Potato Mash

Ingredients:

- 2 large sweet potatoes, peeled and cubed
- 2 tablespoons unsalted butter
- 1/4 cup milk
- 1/4 teaspoon ground cinnamon
- 1/4 teaspoon ground nutmeg
- Salt and pepper to taste

Instructions:

1. Place the sweet potato cubes in a microwave-safe bowl and cover with a microwave-safe lid or plastic wrap, leaving a small vent for steam to escape.
2. Microwave on high for 8-10 minutes, or until the sweet potatoes are tender.
3. Drain any excess liquid and mash the sweet potatoes with a fork or potato masher.
4. Add the butter, milk, cinnamon, nutmeg, salt, and pepper to the bowl and stir to combine.
5. Cover the bowl again and microwave for an additional 2-3 minutes, or until heated through.
6. Remove from the microwave and stir before serving.

Microwaved Cauliflower Fried Rice

Ingredients:

- 1 head cauliflower, grated or pulsed in a food processor
- 2 tablespoons sesame oil
- 2 cloves garlic, minced
- 1 tablespoon grated ginger
- 1/2 cup frozen peas and carrots
- 2 tablespoons soy sauce
- 1/4 teaspoon salt
- 1/4 teaspoon black pepper
- 2 eggs, beaten

Instructions:

1. In a microwave-safe bowl, add the cauliflower, sesame oil, minced garlic, and grated ginger. Toss to coat.
2. Cover the bowl with a microwave-safe lid or plastic wrap, leaving a small vent for steam to escape.
3. Microwave on high for 5-6 minutes, or until the cauliflower is tender.
4. Stir in the frozen peas and carrots, soy sauce, salt, and black pepper.
5. Cover the bowl again and microwave for an additional 2-3 minutes, or until the vegetables are heated through.

6. In a separate microwave-safe bowl, microwave the beaten eggs for 1-2 minutes, stirring every 30 seconds, until fully cooked.

7. Stir the cooked eggs into the cauliflower mixture before serving.

Microwaved Stuffed Bell Peppers

Ingredients:

- 4 large bell peppers, halved and seeded
- 1 pound ground beef
- 1/2 onion, chopped
- 2 garlic cloves, minced
- 1 teaspoon dried oregano
- 1/2 teaspoon salt
- 1/4 teaspoon black pepper
- 1 cup cooked rice
- 1 can (14.5 oz) diced tomatoes
- 1 cup shredded cheddar cheese

Instructions:

1. In a microwave-safe dish, add the bell pepper halves and microwave on high for 3-4 minutes, or until slightly softened.
2. In a microwave-safe bowl, add the ground beef, chopped onion, minced garlic, dried oregano, salt, and black pepper. Microwave on high for 5-6 minutes, or until the beef is browned and cooked through.
3. Drain any excess fat from the beef mixture and stir in the cooked rice and diced tomatoes.
4. Stuff the bell pepper halves with the beef and rice mixture, and sprinkle with shredded cheddar cheese.
5. Cover the dish with a microwave-safe lid or plastic wrap, leaving a small vent for steam to escape.
6. Microwave on high for 5-6 minutes, or until the cheese is melted and the peppers are tender.
7. Remove from the microwave and let cool for a few minutes before serving.

Microwaved Butternut Squash Puree

Ingredients:

- 1 medium butternut squash, peeled, seeded and cubed
- 2 tbsp unsalted butter
- 1/4 cup milk or cream

- 1/4 tsp ground cinnamon
- 1/4 tsp ground nutmeg
- Salt and pepper to taste

Instructions:

1. Place the butternut squash cubes in a microwave-safe bowl, cover it with a microwave-safe lid or plastic wrap and leave a small vent for steam to escape.
2. Microwave on high for 8-10 minutes, or until the butternut squash is tender.
3. Drain any excess liquid and mash the butternut squash with a fork or potato masher.
4. Add butter, milk, cinnamon, nutmeg, salt and pepper to the bowl and stir to combine.
5. Cover the bowl again and microwave for an additional 2-3 minutes, or until heated through.
6. Remove from the microwave, stir and serve.

Microwaved Broccoli and Cheese Casserole

Ingredients:

- 2 cups fresh broccoli florets
- 1 cup shredded cheddar cheese
- 1/2 cup milk or cream
- 1/4 cup all-purpose flour
- 2 tbsp unsalted butter
- Salt and pepper to taste

Instructions:

1. Place the broccoli florets in a microwave-safe bowl, cover with a microwave-safe lid or plastic wrap and leave a small vent for steam to escape.
2. Microwave on high for 2-3 minutes or until the broccoli is tender.
3. In a separate microwave-safe bowl, melt the butter on high for 30 seconds.
4. Stir in the flour, then add the milk gradually, whisking constantly to avoid lumps.
5. Microwave on high for 2-3 minutes, or until the mixture thickens.
6. Add the shredded cheese and stir until melted and smooth.

7. Add the broccoli, salt and pepper to the cheese mixture and stir to combine.
8. Cover the bowl again and microwave for an additional 2-3 minutes, or until heated through and bubbly.
9. Remove from the microwave, stir and serve.

Microwaved Garlic and Herb Green Beans

Ingredients:

*   1 lb fresh green beans, trimmed
*   2 tbsp unsalted butter
*   2 cloves garlic, minced
*   1 tsp dried thyme
*   1 tsp dried rosemary
*   Salt and pepper to taste

Instructions:

1. Place the green beans in a microwave-safe bowl, cover with a microwave-safe lid or plastic wrap and leave a small vent for steam to escape.
2. Microwave on high for 3-4 minutes, or until the green beans are tender.

3. In a separate microwave-safe bowl, melt the butter on high for 30 seconds.
4. Stir in the minced garlic, dried thyme, dried rosemary, salt and pepper.
5. Microwave the garlic herb butter on high for an additional 30-60 seconds, or until fragrant and bubbly.
6. Add the garlic herb butter to the green beans and toss to coat.
7. Cover the bowl again and microwave for an additional 1-2 minutes, or until heated through.
8. Remove from the microwave, stir and serve.

Microwaved Herb-Roasted Carrots

Ingredients:

- 4-5 large carrots, peeled and sliced into thin rounds
- 2 tbsp olive oil
- 2 cloves garlic, minced
- 1 tsp dried thyme
- 1 tsp dried oregano
- Salt and pepper to taste

Instructions:

1. Place the sliced carrots in a microwave-safe bowl, cover with a microwave-safe lid or plastic wrap and leave a small vent for steam to escape.
2. Microwave on high for 5-7 minutes, or until the carrots are tender.
3. In a separate microwave-safe bowl, combine the olive oil, minced garlic, dried thyme, dried oregano, salt and pepper.
4. Microwave the herb mixture on high for 30-60 seconds, or until fragrant.
5. Add the herb mixture to the bowl of cooked carrots and toss to coat.
6. Microwave for an additional 1-2 minutes, or until heated through.
7. Remove from the microwave, stir and serve.

Microwaved Butternut Squash

Ingredients:

- 1 medium butternut squash, peeled and cubed
- 2 tbsp olive oil
- 1 tsp paprika
- 1 tsp garlic powder
- Salt and pepper to taste

Instructions:

1. Place the cubed butternut squash in a microwave-safe bowl and drizzle with olive oil.
2. Sprinkle the paprika, garlic powder, salt and pepper over the squash and toss to coat.
3. Cover the bowl with a microwave-safe lid or plastic wrap and leave a small vent for steam to escape.
4. Microwave on high for 5-7 minutes, or until the squash is tender.
5. Remove from the microwave and stir before serving.

Microwaved Corn on the Cob

Ingredients:

- 4 ears of corn, shucked and cleaned
- 2 tbsp unsalted butter
- Salt and pepper to taste

Instructions:

1. Place the ears of corn in a microwave-safe dish and add enough water to cover the bottom of the dish.
2. Microwave on high for 3-4 minutes per ear of corn.
3. Carefully remove the dish from the microwave and drain any remaining water.
4. Add the butter to the dish and microwave on high for an additional 30-60 seconds, or until the butter is melted.
5. Season the corn with salt and pepper to taste before serving.

Microwaved Roasted Carrots

Ingredients:

- 1 lb carrots, peeled and sliced into sticks
- 2 tbsp olive oil
- 1 tsp paprika
- 1 tsp dried rosemary
- Salt and pepper to taste

Instructions:

1. In a microwave-safe bowl, mix together the olive oil, paprika, dried rosemary, salt, and pepper.
2. Add the sliced carrots to the bowl and toss to coat evenly.
3. Cover the bowl with a microwave-safe lid or plastic wrap and leave a small vent for steam to escape.
4. Microwave on high for 5-7 minutes, or until the carrots are tender.
5. Remove from the microwave, stir, and serve.

Microwaved Parmesan Zucchini

Ingredients:

- 2 medium zucchinis, sliced into rounds
- 1/4 cup grated Parmesan cheese
- 2 tbsp olive oil
- 1 tsp garlic powder
- Salt and pepper to taste

Instructions:

1. In a microwave-safe bowl, mix together the grated Parmesan cheese, olive oil, garlic powder, salt, and pepper.
2. Add the sliced zucchinis to the bowl and toss to coat evenly.
3. Cover the bowl with a microwave-safe lid or plastic wrap and leave a small vent for steam to escape.
4. Microwave on high for 4-6 minutes, or until the zucchinis are tender and the cheese is melted.
5. Remove from the microwave, stir, and serve.

Microwaved Sweet Potato Chips

Ingredients:

- 2 large sweet potatoes, peeled and sliced thinly
- 2 tbsp olive oil
- 1 tsp garlic powder
- Salt and pepper to taste

Instructions:

1. In a microwave-safe bowl, mix together the sliced sweet potatoes, olive oil, garlic powder, salt, and pepper.
2. Toss the sweet potatoes until they are coated evenly.
3. Arrange the sweet potato slices in a single layer on a microwave-safe plate.
4. Microwave on high for 4-6 minutes or until the sweet potatoes are crisp and lightly browned.
5. Carefully remove the plate from the microwave and let cool for a few minutes before serving.

Meat and Poultry

Microwaved Honey Mustard Chicken

Ingredients:

- 4 boneless, skinless chicken breasts
- 1/4 cup honey
- 1/4 cup Dijon mustard
- 1 tbsp olive oil
- 1 tsp garlic powder
- Salt and pepper to taste

Instructions:

1. In a microwave-safe dish, whisk together the honey, Dijon mustard, olive oil, garlic powder, salt, and pepper.
2. Add the chicken breasts to the dish and coat them evenly with the honey mustard mixture.
3. Cover the dish with microwave-safe plastic wrap or a lid and microwave on high for 10-12 minutes or until the chicken is cooked through.
4. Let cool for a few minutes before serving.

Microwaved Meatballs

Ingredients:

- 1 lb ground beef
- 1/2 cup breadcrumbs
- 1/4 cup grated Parmesan cheese
- 1 egg
- 1/4 cup chopped onion
- 1 tsp garlic powder
- 1 tsp dried oregano
- Salt and pepper to taste

Instructions:

1. In a microwave-safe bowl, combine the ground beef, breadcrumbs, grated Parmesan cheese, egg, chopped onion, garlic powder, oregano, salt, and pepper.
2. Mix everything together until well combined.
3. Shape the mixture into small meatballs, about 1 inch in diameter.
4. Place the meatballs in a microwave-safe dish and cover with microwave-safe plastic wrap or a lid.
5. Microwave on high for 5-7 minutes or until the meatballs are cooked through.
6. Let cool for a few minutes before serving.

Microwaved BBQ Pork Ribs

Ingredients:

- 2 lbs pork ribs
- 1 cup BBQ sauce
- 1/4 cup brown sugar
- 1 tbsp apple cider vinegar
- 1 tsp garlic powder
- 1 tsp onion powder
- Salt and pepper to taste

Instructions:

1. In a microwave-safe dish, whisk together the BBQ sauce, brown sugar, apple cider vinegar, garlic powder, onion powder, salt, and pepper.
2. Add the pork ribs to the dish and coat them evenly with the BBQ sauce mixture.
3. Cover the dish with microwave-safe plastic wrap or a lid and microwave on high for 15-20 minutes or until the ribs are cooked through.
4. Remove the plastic wrap or lid and microwave for an additional 5 minutes to allow the BBQ sauce to caramelize on the ribs.
5. Let cool for a few minutes before serving.

Microwaved Lemon Garlic Chicken

Ingredients:

- 4 boneless, skinless chicken breasts
- 2 lemons, juiced and zested
- 2 cloves garlic, minced
- 2 tbsp olive oil
- Salt and pepper to taste

Instructions:

1. In a microwave-safe dish, whisk together the lemon juice, lemon zest, minced garlic, olive oil, salt, and pepper.
2. Add the chicken breasts to the dish and coat them evenly with the lemon garlic mixture.
3. Cover the dish with microwave-safe plastic wrap or a lid and microwave on high for 10-12 minutes or until the chicken is cooked through.
4. Let cool for a few minutes before serving.

Microwaved Teriyaki Chicken

Ingredients:

- 4 boneless, skinless chicken breasts
- 1/2 cup teriyaki sauce
- 1/4 cup honey
- 1/4 cup soy sauce
- 1 tbsp grated ginger
- 1 tbsp cornstarch
- 1 tbsp water
- Green onions and sesame seeds for garnish (optional)

Instructions:

1. In a microwave-safe dish, whisk together the teriyaki sauce, honey, soy sauce, and grated ginger.
2. Add the chicken breasts to the dish and coat them evenly with the teriyaki mixture.
3. Cover the dish with microwave-safe plastic wrap or a lid and microwave on high for 10-12 minutes or until the chicken is cooked through.
4. In a small bowl, whisk together the cornstarch and water. Remove the chicken from the dish and set it aside.
5. Add the cornstarch mixture to the teriyaki sauce in the dish and microwave for an additional 2-3 minutes, stirring occasionally, until the sauce thickens.

6. Pour the sauce over the chicken and garnish with green onions and sesame seeds, if desired.

Microwaved Bacon-Wrapped Pork Tenderloin

Ingredients:

- 1 pork tenderloin, trimmed
- 6 slices bacon
- 1 tbsp Dijon mustard
- 1 tbsp maple syrup
- 1 tbsp soy sauce
- 1 tbsp apple cider vinegar
- Salt and pepper to taste

Instructions:

1. In a microwave-safe dish, whisk together the Dijon mustard, maple syrup, soy sauce, apple cider vinegar, salt, and pepper.
2. Wrap the pork tenderloin with the bacon slices and place it in the dish, seam-side down.
3. Coat the pork evenly with the mustard mixture.

4. Cover the dish with microwave-safe plastic wrap or a lid and microwave on high for 10-12 minutes or until the pork is cooked through and the bacon is crispy.
5. Let cool for a few minutes before slicing and serving.

Microwave Meatballs

Ingredients:

- 1 pound ground beef
- 1/2 cup breadcrumbs
- 1/4 cup milk
- 1 egg
- 1/2 cup grated Parmesan cheese
- 1/2 tsp garlic powder
- 1/2 tsp salt
- 1/4 tsp black pepper
- 1 cup marinara sauce

Instructions:

1. In a large bowl, combine the ground beef, breadcrumbs, milk, egg, Parmesan cheese, garlic powder, salt, and black pepper. Mix well.
2. Form the mixture into 1-inch meatballs and arrange them in a microwave-safe dish.

3. Pour the marinara sauce over the meatballs, making sure they are evenly coated.
4. Cover the dish with microwave-safe plastic wrap or a lid and microwave on high for 8-10 minutes or until the meatballs are cooked through.
5. Let the meatballs cool for a few minutes before serving with additional marinara sauce if desired.

Microwaved Lemon Garlic Chicken Thighs

Ingredients:

- 4 bone-in, skin-on chicken thighs
- 2 cloves garlic, minced
- 2 tbsp olive oil
- 2 tbsp lemon juice
- 1 tsp dried oregano
- 1/2 tsp salt
- 1/4 tsp black pepper
- Lemon wedges for serving (optional)

Instructions:

1. In a small bowl, whisk together the garlic, olive oil, lemon juice, oregano, salt, and black pepper.

2. Arrange the chicken thighs in a single layer in a microwave-safe dish.

3. Pour the garlic and lemon mixture over the chicken, making sure it is evenly coated.

4. Cover the dish with microwave-safe plastic wrap or a lid and microwave on high for 10-12 minutes or until the chicken is cooked through and the skin is crispy.

5. Let the chicken cool for a few minutes before serving with lemon wedges, if desired.

Microwave Chicken Fajitas

Ingredients:

- 1 pound boneless, skinless chicken breast, sliced into strips
- 1 red bell pepper, sliced into strips
- 1 green bell pepper, sliced into strips
- 1 onion, sliced into strips
- 2 tbsp olive oil
- 1 tbsp chili powder
- 1 tsp cumin
- 1/2 tsp garlic powder
- Salt and black pepper to taste
- Flour tortillas

- Toppings (optional): salsa, guacamole, sour cream, shredded cheese

Instructions:

1. In a large microwave-safe dish, combine the chicken, bell peppers, and onion.
2. Drizzle olive oil over the chicken and vegetables and sprinkle with chili powder, cumin, garlic powder, salt, and black pepper. Toss to coat evenly.
3. Cover the dish with microwave-safe plastic wrap or a lid and microwave on high for 8-10 minutes or until the chicken is cooked through and the vegetables are tender.
4. Serve the chicken and vegetables in flour tortillas with your favorite toppings.

Microwaved Turkey Meatloaf

Ingredients:

- 1 pound ground turkey
- 1/2 cup breadcrumbs
- 1/4 cup milk
- 1 egg
- 1/2 cup grated Parmesan cheese

- 1/2 tsp garlic powder
- 1/2 tsp dried oregano
- Salt and black pepper to taste
- 1/2 cup ketchup

Instructions:

1. In a large bowl, combine the ground turkey, breadcrumbs, milk, egg, Parmesan cheese, garlic powder, oregano, salt, and black pepper. Mix well.
2. Form the mixture into a loaf and place it in a microwave-safe dish.
3. Spread ketchup over the top of the meatloaf.
4. Cover the dish with microwave-safe plastic wrap or a lid and microwave on high for 12-15 minutes or until the meatloaf is cooked through.
5. Let the meatloaf cool for a few minutes before slicing and serving.

Microwaved Chicken Teriyaki

Ingredients:

- 2 boneless, skinless chicken breasts
- 1/2 cup soy sauce
- 1/4 cup honey
- 2 tablespoons rice vinegar
- 1 tablespoon sesame oil
- 1 tablespoon grated fresh ginger
- 1 clove garlic, minced
- 1/4 teaspoon black pepper
- 1 tablespoon cornstarch
- 2 tablespoons cold water
- Sesame seeds and sliced green onions for garnish

Instructions:

1. Cut the chicken breasts into bite-sized pieces.
2. In a microwave-safe bowl, whisk together the soy sauce, honey, rice vinegar, sesame oil, grated ginger, minced garlic, and black pepper.
3. Add the chicken to the bowl and stir to coat.
4. Cover the bowl with a microwave-safe lid or plastic wrap and microwave on high for 6 minutes.
5. In a separate bowl, mix together the cornstarch and cold water until smooth.

6. Remove the bowl from the microwave and uncover. Stir the chicken and sauce, then add the cornstarch mixture and stir to combine.
7. Cover the bowl again and microwave for an additional 2-3 minutes, or until the sauce has thickened and the chicken is cooked through.
8. Serve hot, garnished with sesame seeds and sliced green onions.

Microwaved Pork Chops with Mustard

Ingredients:

- 2 bone-in pork chops
- 2 tablespoons Dijon mustard
- 2 tablespoons brown sugar
- 1 tablespoon olive oil
- 1/4 teaspoon salt
- 1/4 teaspoon black pepper
- 1/4 teaspoon smoked paprika

Instructions:

1. In a small bowl, mix together the Dijon mustard, brown sugar, olive oil, salt, black pepper, and smoked paprika to make the glaze.
2. Place the pork chops in a microwave-safe dish and spread the glaze over the tops of the chops.
3. Cover the dish with a microwave-safe lid or plastic wrap and microwave on high for 8-10 minutes, or until the pork chops are cooked through.
4. Remove the dish from the microwave and let the pork chops rest for a few minutes before serving.

Microwave Bacon-Wrapped Meatloaf

Ingredients:

- 1 pound ground beef
- 1/2 cup breadcrumbs
- 1/4 cup ketchup
- 1/4 cup diced onion
- 1 egg
- Salt and pepper, to taste
- 4-6 slices of bacon
- Ketchup (for topping)

Instructions:

1. In a large bowl, mix together ground beef, breadcrumbs, ketchup, diced onion, egg, salt, and pepper until well combined.
2. Divide the meat mixture into 4-6 portions and shape each portion into a mini meatloaf.
3. Wrap each meatloaf with a slice of bacon and place on a microwave-safe dish.
4. Cover with plastic wrap and microwave on high for 12-15 minutes or until the internal temperature reaches 160°F.
5. Remove from the microwave and let the meatloaves rest for 5 minutes before serving with a dollop of ketchup on top.

Microwave Garlic Herb Butter Steak

Ingredients:

- 1 lb. steak (sirloin, ribeye, or strip steak)
- 2 tbsp. butter, softened
- 1 tbsp. minced garlic
- 1 tsp. dried thyme
- 1 tsp. dried rosemary

- Salt and pepper, to taste

Directions:

1. Mix together the softened butter, minced garlic, dried thyme, dried rosemary, salt, and pepper in a small bowl.
2. Rub the mixture all over the steak, making sure to coat both sides evenly.
3. Place the steak on a microwave-safe plate and cover loosely with a piece of wax paper or parchment paper.
4. Microwave on high for 5-7 minutes, depending on the desired doneness of the steak (5 minutes for medium-rare, 7 minutes for medium).
5. Remove from microwave and let the steak rest for a few minutes before slicing and serving.

Microwave BBQ Pork Ribs

Ingredients:

- 1 rack of pork ribs (trimmed and cut into individual ribs)
- 1 cup of BBQ sauce
- 1/4 cup of apple cider vinegar
- 1/4 cup of brown sugar
- 1 tablespoon of paprika
- Salt and pepper to taste

Instructions:

1. In a small bowl, mix together the BBQ sauce, apple cider vinegar, brown sugar, paprika, salt, and pepper.
2. Place the pork ribs in a microwave-safe dish and coat them with the BBQ sauce mixture.
3. Cover the dish with microwave-safe plastic wrap and microwave on high for 10-12 minutes, or until the pork is cooked through and tender.
4. Remove the plastic wrap and brush the pork ribs with additional BBQ sauce.
5. Serve hot with your favorite side dishes.

Microwave Beef Stroganoff

Ingredients:

- 1 lb beef sirloin, sliced into thin strips
- 1 cup sliced mushrooms
- 1 small onion, chopped
- 1 clove garlic, minced
- 1/2 cup beef broth
- 1/2 cup sour cream
- 2 tbsp all-purpose flour
- 2 tbsp butter

- 1 tsp Dijon mustard
- 1 tsp paprika
- Salt and black pepper, to taste

Directions:

1. In a microwave-safe dish, melt the butter on high for 30 seconds.
2. Add the sliced beef, onions, mushrooms, and garlic to the dish and microwave on high for 5-6 minutes, or until the beef is cooked through.
3. In a small bowl, whisk together the beef broth, sour cream, flour, Dijon mustard, paprika, salt, and black pepper.
4. Pour the mixture over the beef and vegetables, and stir to combine.
5. Cover the dish with microwave-safe plastic wrap and microwave on high for an additional 3-4 minutes, or until the sauce thickens.
6. Serve hot over cooked egg noodles or rice.

Microwave Lemon Garlic Butter Chicken

Ingredients:

- 4 boneless chicken breasts
- 2 tablespoons butter
- 1/4 cup lemon juice
- 2 cloves garlic, minced
- Salt and pepper to taste

Instructions:

1. Arrange chicken breasts in a microwave-safe dish.
2. In a microwave-safe bowl, melt butter and stir in lemon juice and garlic.
3. Pour the butter mixture over the chicken breasts.
4. Sprinkle salt and pepper over the chicken.
5. Cover the dish with microwave-safe plastic wrap, leaving one corner open for venting.
6. Microwave on high for 10-12 minutes, or until the chicken is fully cooked.
7. Let the chicken rest for 5 minutes before serving.

Microwave Herb Roasted Pork Tenderloin

Ingredients:

- 1 pound pork tenderloin
- 2 tablespoons olive oil
- 2 tablespoons dried Italian herbs
- 1 teaspoon garlic powder
- Salt and pepper to taste

Instructions:

1. Pat dry the pork tenderloin with paper towels and place it in a microwave-safe dish.
2. In a small bowl, mix together olive oil, Italian herbs, garlic powder, salt, and pepper.
3. Rub the herb mixture all over the pork tenderloin.
4. Cover the dish with microwave-safe plastic wrap, leaving one corner open for venting.
5. Microwave on high for 10-12 minutes, or until the pork tenderloin is fully cooked.
6. Let the pork tenderloin rest for 5 minutes before slicing and serving.

Lemon Garlic Chicken

Ingredients:

- 4 boneless, skinless chicken breasts
- 3 cloves garlic, minced
- 1/4 cup olive oil
- 1/4 cup lemon juice
- 1 teaspoon dried oregano
- Salt and pepper

Directions:

1. Place chicken breasts in a microwave-safe dish.
2. In a small bowl, mix garlic, olive oil, lemon juice, oregano, salt, and pepper.
3. Pour the mixture over the chicken breasts, making sure they are fully coated.
4. Cover the dish with a microwave-safe lid or plastic wrap.
5. Microwave on high for 10-12 minutes, or until the chicken is cooked through.
6. Remove from the microwave and let rest for a few minutes before serving.

BBQ Pork Chops

Ingredients:

- 4 bone-in pork chops
- 1/2 cup BBQ sauce
- 1 tablespoon brown sugar
- 1 tablespoon apple cider vinegar
- 1/2 teaspoon smoked paprika
- Salt and pepper

Directions:

1. Place pork chops in a microwave-safe dish.
2. In a small bowl, mix BBQ sauce, brown sugar, apple cider vinegar, smoked paprika, salt, and pepper.
3. Pour the mixture over the pork chops, making sure they are fully coated.
4. Cover the dish with a microwave-safe lid or plastic wrap.
5. Microwave on high for 10-12 minutes, or until the pork chops are cooked through.
6. Remove from the microwave and let rest for a few minutes before serving.

Microwave BBQ Pulled Pork

Ingredients:

- 1 pound pork shoulder
- 1/4 cup BBQ sauce
- 1/4 cup chicken broth
- 1 tbsp apple cider vinegar
- 1 tsp smoked paprika
- 1 tsp garlic powder
- Salt and pepper to taste

Instructions:

1. Place the pork shoulder in a microwave-safe dish and season with salt and pepper.
2. In a separate bowl, mix together the BBQ sauce, chicken broth, apple cider vinegar, smoked paprika, and garlic powder.
3. Pour the mixture over the pork shoulder and cover the dish with microwave-safe plastic wrap.
4. Microwave on high for 10 minutes, then remove the plastic wrap and stir the meat.
5. Cover the dish again with plastic wrap and microwave for another 10 minutes.
6. Remove the plastic wrap and use two forks to shred the pork.

7. Serve with your favorite side dishes.

Microwave Lemon Herb Chicken

Ingredients:

- 4 boneless, skinless chicken breasts
- 2 tbsp olive oil
- 1 tbsp lemon juice
- 1 tsp dried oregano
- 1 tsp dried thyme
- 1 tsp garlic powder
- Salt and pepper to taste

Instructions:

1. In a small bowl, mix together the olive oil, lemon juice, oregano, thyme, garlic powder, salt, and pepper.
2. Place the chicken breasts in a microwave-safe dish and brush the herb mixture over them.
3. Cover the dish with microwave-safe plastic wrap.
4. Microwave on high for 5 minutes, then remove the plastic wrap and flip the chicken over.
5. Brush the remaining herb mixture over the chicken and cover the dish with plastic wrap again.

6. Microwave on high for another 5 minutes, or until the chicken is cooked through.
7. Let the chicken rest for a few minutes before serving.

Microwaved Lemon-Garlic Chicken

Ingredients:

- 4 boneless, skinless chicken breasts
- 1/4 cup olive oil
- 1/4 cup lemon juice
- 2 cloves garlic, minced
- 1 tsp dried oregano
- 1/2 tsp salt
- 1/4 tsp black pepper

Directions:

1. In a small bowl, whisk together olive oil, lemon juice, garlic, oregano, salt, and black pepper.
2. Place chicken breasts in a microwave-safe dish and pour the marinade over the chicken, making sure to coat each piece.
3. Cover the dish with plastic wrap and microwave on high for 5-6 minutes, or until the chicken is cooked through.
4. Let the chicken rest for 2-3 minutes before serving.

Microwaved Beef and Broccoli Stir-Fry

Ingredients:

- 1 lb flank steak, thinly sliced
- 2 cups broccoli florets
- 1/4 cup soy sauce
- 2 cloves garlic, minced
- 1 tbsp honey
- 1 tbsp cornstarch
- 1/4 tsp black pepper
- 1 tbsp vegetable oil
- Cooked rice, for serving

Directions:

1. In a microwave-safe dish, whisk together soy sauce, garlic, honey, cornstarch, and black pepper.
2. Add sliced flank steak to the dish and toss to coat in the sauce.
3. Add broccoli florets to the dish, placing them on top of the beef.
4. Drizzle vegetable oil over the top of the broccoli.
5. Cover the dish with plastic wrap and microwave on high for 6-7 minutes, or until the beef is cooked through and the broccoli is tender.
6. Serve over cooked rice.

Microwave Garlic Butter Steak

Ingredients:

- 1 (8-ounce) steak
- 1 tablespoon butter
- 1 teaspoon minced garlic
- Salt and pepper to taste
- Fresh parsley (optional)

Instructions:

1. Season the steak with salt and pepper.
2. In a microwave-safe dish, melt the butter and garlic together for 20 seconds.
3. Add the steak to the dish and spoon the garlic butter over the top.
4. Microwave on high for 4-6 minutes, or until the internal temperature of the steak reaches 135°F (57°C) for medium-rare or 145°F (63°C) for medium.
5. Let the steak rest for 5 minutes before slicing and serving. Garnish with fresh parsley, if desired.

Fish & Seafood

Microwave Shrimp Scampi

Ingredients:

- 1/2 pound of shrimp, peeled and deveined
- 2 tablespoons of butter
- 2 garlic cloves, minced
- 1 tablespoon of lemon juice
- Salt and black pepper, to taste
- 2 tablespoons of chopped fresh parsley

Instructions:

1. In a microwave-safe dish, melt the butter and garlic on high for 30 seconds.
2. Add the shrimp to the dish and toss to coat them in the butter mixture.
3. Microwave the shrimp on high for 2-3 minutes or until they turn pink and are cooked through.
4. Remove the dish from the microwave and add lemon juice, salt, black pepper, and chopped parsley to the shrimp.
5. Serve the shrimp scampi with a side of rice or pasta.

Microwave Salmon with Vegetables

Ingredients:

- 4 salmon fillets
- 1 cup of broccoli florets
- 1 cup of sliced carrots
- 1/2 cup of sliced red onion
- 2 tablespoons of olive oil
- Salt and black pepper, to taste
- 2 tablespoons of soy sauce

Instructions:

1. In a microwave-safe dish, combine the broccoli, carrots, and red onion. Drizzle with olive oil and season with salt and black pepper.
2. Microwave the vegetables on high for 2-3 minutes or until they are slightly tender.
3. Add the salmon fillets on top of the vegetables and season them with salt and black pepper.
4. Drizzle the soy sauce over the salmon and vegetables.
5. Microwave the dish on high for 5-6 minutes or until the salmon is cooked through and flakes easily with a fork.
6. Serve the salmon with the vegetables and drizzle the sauce from the dish over the top.

Microwave Teriyaki Salmon

Ingredients:

- 4 salmon fillets
- 1/4 cup of soy sauce
- 1/4 cup of brown sugar
- 2 tablespoons of honey
- 2 tablespoons of rice vinegar
- 1 tablespoon of grated ginger
- 2 garlic cloves, minced
- 1 tablespoon of sesame seeds

Instructions:

1. In a microwave-safe dish, combine the soy sauce, brown sugar, honey, rice vinegar, grated ginger, and minced garlic. Stir until the sugar is dissolved.
2. Add the salmon fillets to the dish and spoon the sauce over the top.
3. Microwave the dish on high for 5-6 minutes or until the salmon is cooked through and flakes easily with a fork.
4. Sprinkle sesame seeds over the top of the salmon.
5. Serve the teriyaki salmon with a side of steamed vegetables or rice.

Microwave Scallop Risotto

Ingredients:

- 1 cup of Arborio rice
- 2 cups of chicken or seafood stock
- 1/4 cup of white wine
- 1/4 cup of diced onion
- 1/2 cup of diced mushrooms
- 1/2 pound of scallops
- 2 tablespoons of butter
- Salt and black pepper, to taste
- 1/4 cup of grated Parmesan cheese

Instructions:

1. In a microwave-safe dish, combine the Arborio rice, chicken or seafood stock, white wine, diced onion, and diced mushrooms.
2. Microwave the dish on high for 12-15 minutes or until the rice is cooked and the liquid is absorbed.
3. Add the scallops to the dish and microwave for an additional 2-3 minutes or until the scallops are cooked through.
4. Stir in the butter, salt, black pepper, and grated Parmesan cheese until the risotto is creamy and smooth.

5. Serve the scallop risotto with a side of steamed vegetables or a salad.

Microwave Tuna and Vegetable Casserole

Ingredients:

- 2 cans of tuna, drained
- 1/2 cup of diced onion
- 1/2 cup of diced bell pepper
- 1/2 cup of diced zucchini
- 1/2 cup of diced tomato
- 1/2 cup of mayonnaise
- 1/4 cup of sour cream
- 1/4 cup of grated Parmesan cheese
- Salt and black pepper, to taste

Instructions:

1. In a microwave-safe dish, combine the drained tuna, diced onion, diced bell pepper, diced zucchini, and diced tomato.
2. Microwave the dish on high for 5-6 minutes or until the vegetables are tender.

3. In a small bowl, mix together the mayonnaise, sour cream, grated Parmesan cheese, salt, and black pepper.
4. Pour the mayonnaise mixture over the tuna and vegetables and stir until everything is coated evenly.
5. Microwave the dish on high for an additional 2-3 minutes or until the casserole is heated through.
6. Serve the tuna and vegetable casserole with a side of crusty bread or a salad.

Microwave Shrimp Alfredo

Ingredients:

- 1 pound of cooked shrimp, peeled and deveined
- 8 ounces of fettuccine pasta
- 2 tablespoons of butter
- 2 garlic cloves, minced
- 1 cup of heavy cream
- 1/2 cup of grated Parmesan cheese
- Salt and black pepper, to taste
- 1 tablespoon of chopped fresh parsley

Instructions:

1. Cook the fettuccine pasta according to package instructions and drain.

2. In a microwave-safe dish, melt the butter and minced garlic on high for 1-2 minutes.
3. Add the heavy cream and grated Parmesan cheese to the dish and microwave on high for 2-3 minutes or until the cheese is melted and the sauce is heated through.
4. Add the cooked shrimp and cooked fettuccine to the dish and stir until everything is coated in the sauce.
5. Microwave the dish on high for an additional 2-3 minutes or until the shrimp and pasta are heated through.
6. Sprinkle chopped fresh parsley over the top of the shrimp alfredo before serving.

Microwave Lemon Pepper Salmon

Ingredients:

- 4 salmon fillets
- 2 tablespoons of butter
- 2 garlic cloves, minced
- 2 tablespoons of lemon juice
- 1 tablespoon of lemon zest
- 1/2 teaspoon of black pepper
- Salt, to taste

Instructions:

1. In a microwave-safe dish, melt the butter and minced garlic on high for 1-2 minutes.
2. Add the lemon juice, lemon zest, black pepper, and salt to the dish and stir until everything is combined.
3. Add the salmon fillets to the dish and spoon the lemon pepper sauce over the top of each fillet.
4. Microwave the dish on high for 5-6 minutes or until the salmon is cooked through and flakes easily with a fork.
5. Serve the lemon pepper salmon with a side of steamed vegetables or rice.

Microwave Cajun Shrimp and Rice

Ingredients:

- 1 pound of shrimp, peeled and deveined
- 1 cup of uncooked white rice
- 1 can of diced tomatoes, drained
- 1 green bell pepper, diced
- 1 onion, diced
- 2 garlic cloves, minced
- 2 tablespoons of olive oil
- 1 tablespoon of Cajun seasoning
- Salt and black pepper, to taste

- Chopped parsley, for garnish

Instructions:

1. In a microwave-safe dish, combine the rice, diced tomatoes, green bell pepper, onion, minced garlic, olive oil, and Cajun seasoning. Stir to combine.
2. Add enough water to the dish to cover the rice mixture by 1 inch.
3. Microwave the dish on high for 15 minutes or until the rice is cooked and the water has been absorbed.
4. Add the shrimp to the dish and stir to combine.
5. Microwave the dish on high for an additional 2-3 minutes or until the shrimp are pink and cooked through.
6. Season with salt and black pepper to taste.
7. Garnish with chopped parsley before serving.

Microwave Honey Glazed Salmon

Ingredients:

- 4 salmon fillets
- 2 tablespoons of honey
- 2 tablespoons of soy sauce

- 1 tablespoon of rice vinegar
- 2 garlic cloves, minced
- Salt and black pepper, to taste
- Sesame seeds, for garnish

Instructions:

1. In a microwave-safe dish, whisk together the honey, soy sauce, rice vinegar, minced garlic, salt, and black pepper.
2. Add the salmon fillets to the dish and spoon the honey glaze over the top of each fillet.
3. Microwave the dish on high for 5-6 minutes or until the salmon is cooked through and flakes easily with a fork.
4. Garnish with sesame seeds before serving. Serve with steamed vegetables or rice, if desired.

Microwave Lemon Garlic Shrimp Scampi

Ingredients:

- 1 pound of large shrimp, peeled and deveined
- 8 ounces of linguine pasta
- 2 tablespoons of butter
- 2 garlic cloves, minced
- 1/4 cup of chicken broth
- 1/4 cup of white wine

- 2 tablespoons of lemon juice
- 1 teaspoon of lemon zest
- Salt and black pepper, to taste
- Chopped parsley, for garnish

Instructions:

1. Cook the linguine pasta according to package instructions and drain.
2. In a microwave-safe dish, melt the butter and minced garlic on high for 1-2 minutes.
3. Add the chicken broth, white wine, lemon juice, and lemon zest to the dish and stir until everything is combined.
4. Add the shrimp and cooked linguine to the dish and stir until everything is coated in the sauce.
5. Microwave the dish on high for 3-4 minutes or until the shrimp are pink and cooked through.
6. Season with salt and black pepper to taste.
7. Garnish with chopped parsley before serving.

Microwave Coconut Curry Shrimp

Ingredients:

- 1 pound of large shrimp, peeled and deveined

- 1 can of coconut milk
- 2 tablespoons of red curry paste
- 1 tablespoon of brown sugar
- 1 tablespoon of fish sauce
- 1 tablespoon of lime juice
- 1 red bell pepper, sliced
- 1 small onion, sliced
- Salt and black pepper, to taste
- Chopped cilantro, for garnish

Instructions:

1. In a microwave-safe dish, whisk together the coconut milk, red curry paste, brown sugar, fish sauce, and lime juice.
2. Add the sliced red bell pepper and onion to the dish and stir until they are coated in the curry mixture.
3. Microwave the dish on high for 4-5 minutes or until the vegetables are tender.
4. Add the shrimp to the dish and stir until they are coated in the curry mixture.
5. Microwave the dish on high for 2-3 minutes or until the shrimp are pink and cooked through.
6. Season with salt and black pepper to taste.
7. Garnish with chopped cilantro before serving.

Microwave Lemon Garlic Tilapia

Ingredients:

- 4 tilapia fillets
- 2 tablespoons of butter
- 2 garlic cloves, minced
- 1 tablespoon of lemon juice
- 1 teaspoon of lemon zest
- Salt and black pepper, to taste
- Chopped parsley, for garnish

Instructions:

1. In a microwave-safe dish, melt the butter and minced garlic on high for 1-2 minutes.
2. Add the lemon juice and lemon zest to the dish and stir until everything is combined.
3. Add the tilapia fillets to the dish and spoon the lemon garlic sauce over the top of each fillet.
4. Microwave the dish on high for 5-6 minutes or until the tilapia is cooked through and flakes easily with a fork.
5. Season with salt and black pepper to taste.
6. Garnish with chopped parsley before serving. Serve with steamed vegetables or rice, if desired.

Microwave Cajun Salmon

Ingredients:

- 4 salmon fillets
- 2 tablespoons of olive oil
- 2 teaspoons of Cajun seasoning
- Salt and black pepper, to taste
- Lemon wedges, for garnish

Instructions:

1. In a microwave-safe dish, brush the salmon fillets with olive oil.
2. Sprinkle the Cajun seasoning evenly over the top of each fillet.
3. Season with salt and black pepper to taste.
4. Microwave the dish on high for 5-6 minutes or until the salmon is cooked through and flakes easily with a fork.
5. Garnish with lemon wedges before serving.

Microwave Teriyaki Glazed Salmon

Ingredients:

- 4 salmon fillets
- 1/4 cup of soy sauce
- 2 tablespoons of honey
- 1 tablespoon of rice vinegar
- 1 tablespoon of sesame oil
- 1 tablespoon of grated ginger
- 2 garlic cloves, minced
- Salt and black pepper, to taste
- Sesame seeds and sliced scallions, for garnish

Instructions:

1. In a microwave-safe dish, whisk together the soy sauce, honey, rice vinegar, sesame oil, grated ginger, and minced garlic.
2. Place the salmon fillets in the dish, skin-side down, and spoon some of the teriyaki sauce over the top.
3. Season with salt and black pepper to taste.
4. Microwave the dish on high for 5-6 minutes or until the salmon is cooked through and flakes easily with a fork.
5. Spoon some of the remaining teriyaki sauce over the top of the cooked salmon and sprinkle with sesame seeds and sliced scallions before serving.

Microwave Coconut Curry Shrimp

Ingredients:

- 1 pound of large shrimp, peeled and deveined
- 1 can of coconut milk
- 2 tablespoons of red curry paste
- 2 garlic cloves, minced
- 1 tablespoon of grated ginger
- 1 tablespoon of fish sauce
- 1 tablespoon of brown sugar
- Salt and black pepper, to taste
- Chopped cilantro and lime wedges, for garnish

Instructions:

1. In a microwave-safe dish, whisk together the coconut milk, red curry paste, minced garlic, grated ginger, fish sauce, and brown sugar.
2. Add the shrimp to the dish and toss to coat in the curry sauce.
3. Season with salt and black pepper to taste.
4. Microwave the dish on high for 3-4 minutes or until the shrimp are pink and cooked through.
5. Garnish with chopped cilantro and lime wedges before serving. Serve with steamed rice, if desired.

Microwave Lemon Butter Cod

Ingredients:

- 4 cod fillets
- 1/4 cup of butter, melted
- 1 tablespoon of lemon juice
- 1 teaspoon of minced garlic
- 1/2 teaspoon of dried thyme
- Salt and black pepper, to taste
- Lemon wedges, for garnish

Instructions:

1. In a microwave-safe dish, whisk together the melted butter, lemon juice, minced garlic, and dried thyme.
2. Add the cod fillets to the dish and spoon the lemon butter sauce over the top.
3. Season with salt and black pepper to taste.
4. Microwave the dish on high for 6-7 minutes or until the cod is cooked through and flakes easily with a fork.
5. Garnish with lemon wedges before serving.

Microwave Cajun Shrimp and Rice

Ingredients:

- 1 pound of large shrimp, peeled and deveined
- 1 cup of uncooked white rice
- 1 can of diced tomatoes, drained
- 1 onion, chopped
- 1 green bell pepper, chopped
- 1 tablespoon of Cajun seasoning
- 2 garlic cloves, minced
- 2 cups of chicken broth
- Salt and black pepper, to taste
- Chopped parsley, for garnish

Instructions:

1. In a microwave-safe dish, combine the uncooked rice, diced tomatoes, chopped onion, chopped green bell pepper, Cajun seasoning, minced garlic, and chicken broth.
2. Microwave the dish on high for 12-14 minutes or until the rice is cooked and the liquid is absorbed.
3. Add the shrimp to the dish and stir to combine.
4. Microwave the dish on high for 3-4 minutes or until the shrimp are pink and cooked through.
5. Season with salt and black pepper to taste.

6. Garnish with chopped parsley before serving.

Microwave Garlic and Herb Salmon

Ingredients:

- 4 salmon fillets
- 2 tablespoons of butter, melted
- 2 garlic cloves, minced
- 1 teaspoon of dried thyme
- 1 teaspoon of dried oregano
- Salt and black pepper, to taste
- Lemon wedges, for garnish

Instructions:

1. In a microwave-safe dish, whisk together the melted butter, minced garlic, dried thyme, and dried oregano.
2. Add the salmon fillets to the dish and spoon the garlic herb mixture over the top.
3. Season with salt and black pepper to taste.
4. Microwave the dish on high for 6-7 minutes or until the salmon is cooked through and flakes easily with a fork.
5. Garnish with lemon wedges before serving.

Microwave Teriyaki Shrimp Stir-Fry

Ingredients:

- 1 pound of large shrimp, peeled and deveined
- 1 tablespoon of vegetable oil
- 1 red bell pepper, sliced
- 1 green bell pepper, sliced
- 1 onion, sliced
- 2 garlic cloves, minced
- 1/4 cup of teriyaki sauce
- 1 tablespoon of cornstarch
- Salt and black pepper, to taste
- Sesame seeds and sliced green onions, for garnish

Instructions:

1. In a microwave-safe dish, toss together the shrimp, vegetable oil, sliced red and green bell peppers, sliced onion, and minced garlic.
2. Microwave the dish on high for 6-7 minutes or until the shrimp is pink and cooked through.
3. In a small bowl, whisk together the teriyaki sauce and cornstarch.
4. Add the teriyaki mixture to the dish and stir to combine.
5. Microwave the dish on high for an additional 1-2 minutes or until the sauce has thickened.

6. Season with salt and black pepper to taste.
7. Garnish with sesame seeds and sliced green onions before serving.

Microwave Thai Coconut Curry Cod

Ingredients:

- 4 cod fillets
- 1 can of coconut milk
- 2 tablespoons of red curry paste
- 1 tablespoon of fish sauce
- 1 tablespoon of brown sugar
- 1 red bell pepper, sliced
- 1 green bell pepper, sliced
- 1 onion, sliced
- 2 garlic cloves, minced
- Salt and black pepper, to taste
- Fresh cilantro leaves, for garnish

Instructions:

1. In a microwave-safe dish, whisk together the coconut milk, red curry paste, fish sauce, and brown sugar.
2. Add the cod fillets to the dish and spoon the coconut curry mixture over the top.

3. Add the sliced red and green bell peppers, sliced onion, and minced garlic to the dish.
4. Season with salt and black pepper to taste.
5. Microwave the dish on high for 8-10 minutes or until the cod is cooked through and flakes easily with a fork.
6. Garnish with fresh cilantro leaves before serving.

Microwave Lemon Herb Tilapia

Ingredients:

- 4 tilapia fillets
- 2 tablespoons of butter, melted
- 2 garlic cloves, minced
- Juice of 1 lemon
- 1 teaspoon of dried thyme
- 1 teaspoon of dried rosemary
- Salt and black pepper, to taste
- Lemon slices and fresh parsley, for garnish

Instructions:

1. In a microwave-safe dish, whisk together the melted butter, minced garlic, lemon juice, dried thyme, and dried rosemary.

2. Add the tilapia fillets to the dish and spoon the lemon herb mixture over the top.
3. Season with salt and black pepper to taste.
4. Microwave the dish on high for 5-6 minutes or until the tilapia is cooked through and flakes easily with a fork.
5. Garnish with lemon slices and fresh parsley before serving.

Microwave Garlic Butter Shrimp

Ingredients:

- 1 pound of large shrimp, peeled and deveined
- 1/4 cup of butter, melted
- 3 garlic cloves, minced
- Juice of 1/2 lemon
- Salt and black pepper, to taste
- Chopped fresh parsley, for garnish

Instructions:

1. In a microwave-safe dish, whisk together the melted butter, minced garlic, and lemon juice.
2. Add the shrimp to the dish and toss to coat in the garlic butter mixture.
3. Season with salt and black pepper to taste.

4. Microwave the dish on high for 3-4 minutes or until the shrimp are cooked through and pink.
5. Garnish with chopped fresh parsley before serving.

Microwave Soy-Ginger Salmon

Ingredients:

- 4 salmon fillets
- 1/4 cup of soy sauce
- 2 tablespoons of honey
- 2 tablespoons of rice vinegar
- 1 tablespoon of minced fresh ginger
- 1 garlic clove, minced
- Sesame seeds and sliced green onions, for garnish

Instructions:

1. In a microwave-safe dish, whisk together the soy sauce, honey, rice vinegar, minced ginger, and minced garlic.
2. Add the salmon fillets to the dish and spoon the soy-ginger mixture over the top.
3. Microwave the dish on high for 5-6 minutes or until the salmon is cooked through and flakes easily with a fork.

4. Garnish with sesame seeds and sliced green onions
    before serving.

Desserts

Microwave Chocolate Mug Cake

Ingredients:

- 4 tablespoons of all-purpose flour
- 4 tablespoons of granulated sugar
- 2 tablespoons of unsweetened cocoa powder
- 1/4 teaspoon of baking powder
- 1/4 cup of milk
- 2 tablespoons of vegetable oil
- 1/4 teaspoon of vanilla extract
- Pinch of salt
- Whipped cream and chocolate chips, for garnish

Instructions:

1. In a microwave-safe mug, whisk together the flour, sugar, cocoa powder, baking powder, and salt until well combined.
2. Add the milk, vegetable oil, and vanilla extract to the mug and stir until smooth.
3. Microwave the mug on high for 1-2 minutes or until the cake is cooked through and set.
4. Garnish with whipped cream and chocolate chips before serving.

Microwave Apple Crisp

Ingredients:

- 2 apples, peeled and diced
- 1/4 cup of all-purpose flour
- 1/4 cup of brown sugar
- 1/4 cup of rolled oats
- 1/4 teaspoon of ground cinnamon
- 2 tablespoons of unsalted butter, softened
- Vanilla ice cream, for serving

Instructions:

1. In a microwave-safe dish, toss together the diced apples, flour, brown sugar, rolled oats, and ground cinnamon.
2. Add the softened butter to the dish and use your fingers to work it into the mixture until it forms coarse crumbs.
3. Microwave the dish on high for 5-7 minutes or until the apples are tender and the topping is golden brown.
4. Let the apple crisp cool for a few minutes before serving with vanilla ice cream.

Microwave Lemon Curd

Ingredients:

- 3/4 cup of granulated sugar
- 2 large eggs
- 2 large egg yolks
- 1/2 cup of fresh lemon juice
- 1/4 cup of unsalted butter, cut into small pieces
- 1 tablespoon of finely grated lemon zest

Instructions:

1. In a large microwave-safe bowl, whisk together the sugar, eggs, egg yolks, and lemon juice until well combined.
2. Add the butter and lemon zest to the bowl and microwave on high for 1 minute.
3. Remove the bowl from the microwave and stir the mixture well.
4. Microwave the mixture on high for another minute and stir well.
5. Continue microwaving the mixture for 30-second intervals, stirring well after each interval, until it thickens and coats the back of a spoon.
6. Pour the lemon curd into a clean jar and let it cool before serving.

Microwave Rice Pudding

Ingredients:

- 1/2 cup of short-grain rice
- 1/4 teaspoon of salt
- 2 cups of milk
- 1/4 cup of granulated sugar
- 1/2 teaspoon of vanilla extract
- Ground cinnamon, for garnish

Instructions:

1. In a large microwave-safe bowl, combine the rice, salt, and milk.
2. Microwave the mixture on high for 10-12 minutes, stirring every few minutes, until the rice is tender and the mixture is thick and creamy.
3. Stir in the sugar and vanilla extract and microwave for another 2-3 minutes until the sugar has dissolved and the pudding is heated through.
4. Let the rice pudding cool for a few minutes before serving, garnished with a sprinkle of ground cinnamon.

Microwave Apple Crisp II

Ingredients:

- 2 medium apples, peeled and diced
- 2 tablespoons of all-purpose flour
- 2 tablespoons of granulated sugar
- 1/4 teaspoon of cinnamon
- 1 tablespoon of unsalted butter, cut into small pieces
- 1/4 cup of old-fashioned oats
- 1/4 cup of chopped pecans

Instructions:

1. In a large microwave-safe bowl, mix together the diced apples, flour, sugar, and cinnamon.
2. Microwave the mixture on high for 3 minutes, stirring every minute, until the apples are tender.
3. In a separate bowl, mix together the butter, oats, and pecans until crumbly.
4. Sprinkle the oat mixture over the apples in the bowl.
5. Microwave the mixture on high for another 2-3 minutes, until the topping is golden brown and crisp.
6. Let the apple crisp cool for a few minutes before serving.

Microwave Lemon Bars

Ingredients:

- 1/2 cup of all-purpose flour
- 1/4 cup of granulated sugar
- 1/4 cup of unsalted butter, softened
- 1 egg yolk
- 1/4 cup of fresh lemon juice
- 1 tablespoon of lemon zest
- 1/4 cup of powdered sugar

Instructions:

1. In a medium bowl, mix together the flour and granulated sugar.
2. Add the softened butter and use a fork or pastry cutter to combine until the mixture is crumbly.
3. Press the mixture evenly into a microwave-safe dish.
4. Microwave on high for 1 minute and 30 seconds.
5. In a separate bowl, whisk together the egg yolk, lemon juice, and lemon zest.
6. Pour the lemon mixture over the crust and microwave on high for another 1 minute and 30 seconds.

7. Let the bars cool completely before dusting with powdered sugar and cutting into squares.

Microwave Banana Bread

Ingredients:

- 1 ripe banana, mashed
- 1/4 cup of all-purpose flour
- 1/4 cup of rolled oats
- 1/4 cup of granulated sugar
- 1/4 teaspoon of baking powder
- 1/4 teaspoon of cinnamon
- 1 egg
- 2 tablespoons of vegetable oil
- 1/4 teaspoon of vanilla extract

Instructions:

1. In a medium bowl, mix together the mashed banana, flour, oats, sugar, baking powder, and cinnamon.
2. In a separate bowl, whisk together the egg, vegetable oil, and vanilla extract.
3. Pour the wet ingredients into the bowl with the dry ingredients and stir until combined.

4. Pour the batter into a microwave-safe dish and microwave on high for 2-3 minutes, until a toothpick inserted in the center comes out clean.

5. Let the banana bread cool for a few minutes before slicing and serving. Optional toppings include sliced bananas, chopped nuts, or a drizzle of honey.

Microwave Brownies

Ingredients:

- 1/2 cup all-purpose flour
- 1/2 cup granulated sugar
- 1/4 cup unsweetened cocoa powder
- 1/4 teaspoon salt
- 1/4 cup vegetable oil
- 2 large eggs
- 1 teaspoon vanilla extract
- 1/4 cup semisweet chocolate chips

Directions:

1. In a large microwave-safe bowl, whisk together the flour, sugar, cocoa powder, and salt.

2. Add the vegetable oil, eggs, and vanilla extract to the dry ingredients and whisk until well combined.

3. Stir in the chocolate chips.
4. Microwave the batter on high for 2-3 minutes or until the top is set and the edges are starting to pull away from the sides of the bowl.
5. Let the brownies cool for a few minutes before slicing and serving.

Microwave Apple Crisp

Ingredients:

- 2 large apples, peeled and sliced
- 1/4 cup all-purpose flour
- 1/4 cup brown sugar
- 1/4 cup quick-cooking oats
- 1/2 teaspoon cinnamon
- 1/4 cup unsalted butter, softened

Directions:

1. In a medium bowl, mix together the flour, brown sugar, oats, and cinnamon.
2. Add the butter and use a fork to mix until the mixture is crumbly.
3. Place the sliced apples in a microwave-safe dish.

4. Sprinkle the crumb mixture over the apples.
5. Microwave on high for 5-7 minutes or until the apples are tender and the topping is golden brown.
6. Let the apple crisp cool for a few minutes before serving.

Microwave Chocolate Lava Cake

Ingredients:

- 1/4 cup all-purpose flour
- 1/4 cup granulated sugar
- 2 tbsp unsweetened cocoa powder
- 1/4 tsp baking powder
- 1/4 cup milk
- 2 tbsp vegetable oil
- 1/4 tsp vanilla extract
- 1 tbsp semi-sweet chocolate chips
- Powdered sugar, for dusting

Instructions:

1. In a microwave-safe mug, whisk together the flour, sugar, cocoa powder, and baking powder.
2. Add in the milk, vegetable oil, and vanilla extract, and whisk until the batter is smooth.
3. Fold in the chocolate chips.

4. Microwave on high for 45-60 seconds, or until the cake is set on top but still gooey in the center.
5. Dust with powdered sugar and serve warm.

Microwave Apple Crisp

Ingredients:

*   1 medium apple, peeled and diced
*   2 tbsp all-purpose flour
*   2 tbsp rolled oats
*   2 tbsp brown sugar
*   1/4 tsp ground cinnamon
*   1 tbsp unsalted butter, softened
*   Vanilla ice cream (optional)

Instructions:

1. In a microwave-safe bowl, mix together the apple, flour, oats, brown sugar, cinnamon, and butter until everything is well combined.
2. Microwave on high for 3-4 minutes, or until the apple is tender and the topping is crisp and golden.
3. Serve warm, with a scoop of vanilla ice cream if desired.

Microwave Fruit Crisp

Ingredients:

- 1 cup mixed fruit (such as berries, peaches, and/or apples), sliced
- 2 tablespoons all-purpose flour
- 2 tablespoons rolled oats
- 2 tablespoons brown sugar
- 1/4 teaspoon ground cinnamon
- 1 tablespoon butter, melted

Instructions:

1. In a microwave-safe bowl, toss together the mixed fruit and flour.
2. In a separate bowl, mix together the oats, brown sugar, and cinnamon.
3. Stir in the melted butter to the oat mixture until crumbly.
4. Sprinkle the oat mixture on top of the fruit.
5. Microwave the bowl on high for 3-4 minutes, until the fruit is tender and the topping is golden brown.
6. Let the crisp cool for a few minutes before serving.

Microwave Apple Crisp

Ingredients:

- 2 cups chopped apples
- 2 tablespoons flour
- 2 tablespoons brown sugar
- 1 tablespoon butter
- 1/4 cup quick-cooking oats
- 1/4 teaspoon cinnamon
- Whipped cream (optional)

Instructions:

1. In a microwave-safe dish, combine the chopped apples, flour, and brown sugar.
2. Mix until the apples are evenly coated.
3. Cut the butter into small pieces and sprinkle over the apple mixture.
4. In a separate bowl, mix together the quick-cooking oats and cinnamon.
5. Sprinkle the oat mixture over the top of the apples.
6. Microwave on high for 3-5 minutes or until the apples are tender and the oat topping is crispy.
7. Top with whipped cream if desired and enjoy!

Microwave Rice Pudding

Ingredients:

- 1/4 cup uncooked white rice
- 1/2 cup water
- 1 cup milk
- 1/4 cup sugar
- 1/4 teaspoon vanilla extract
- Ground cinnamon (optional)

Instructions:

1. In a microwave-safe dish, combine the uncooked rice and water.
2. Microwave on high for 5-6 minutes or until the rice is tender and the water has been absorbed.
3. Add the milk, sugar, and vanilla extract to the dish and stir well.
4. Microwave on high for 3-5 minutes or until the pudding thickens and begins to bubble.
5. Remove from the microwave and sprinkle with ground cinnamon if desired.
6. Serve warm or chilled and enjoy!

Lemon Blueberry Microwave Mug Cake

Ingredients:

- 1/4 cup flour
- 1/4 tsp baking powder
- 1/8 tsp salt
- 1/4 cup granulated sugar
- 2 tbsp unsalted butter, melted
- 1/4 cup milk
- 1/2 tsp lemon zest
- 1 tbsp lemon juice
- 1/4 cup fresh blueberries

Instructions:

1. In a microwave-safe mug, whisk together the flour, baking powder, salt, and sugar.
2. Add the melted butter, milk, lemon zest, and lemon juice to the mug and whisk until smooth.
3. Gently fold in the blueberries.
4. Microwave on high for 1 minute and 30 seconds or until the cake is set and cooked through.
5. Let the cake cool for a few minutes before serving.

Microwave Caramel Custard Pudding

Ingredients:

- 2 eggs
- 1/4 cup granulated sugar
- 1/4 tsp vanilla extract
- 1 1/4 cups milk
- 1/4 cup caramel sauce (store-bought or homemade)

Instructions:

1. In a microwave-safe bowl, whisk together the eggs, sugar, and vanilla extract until well combined.
2. Slowly whisk in the milk until fully incorporated.
3. Pour the caramel sauce into a microwave-safe dish or ramekin.
4. Pour the egg mixture on top of the caramel sauce.
5. Microwave on high for 5-6 minutes or until the custard is set.
6. Let the pudding cool for a few minutes before serving.
7. To serve, invert the pudding onto a plate so that the caramel sauce is on top.

Lemon Berry Microwave Cobbler

Ingredients:

- 1/2 cup of fresh or frozen mixed berries
- 1 tablespoon of granulated sugar
- 1/2 tablespoon of cornstarch
- 1/2 tablespoon of lemon juice
- 1/4 cup of all-purpose flour
- 1 tablespoon of granulated sugar
- 1/4 teaspoon of baking powder
- 1/8 teaspoon of salt
- 1 tablespoon of unsalted butter, melted
- 1 tablespoon of milk

Instructions:

1. In a microwave-safe bowl, mix the berries, 1 tablespoon of sugar, cornstarch, and lemon juice together.
2. Microwave the berry mixture for 1 minute on high. Remove from the microwave and stir.
3. In a separate bowl, mix the flour, 1 tablespoon of sugar, baking powder, and salt together.
4. Add the melted butter and milk to the dry ingredients and stir until just combined.
5. Spoon the batter over the berry mixture.

6. Microwave for 1-2 minutes on high, or until the batter is cooked through and the berry mixture is bubbly.
7. Serve warm with a dollop of whipped cream or vanilla ice cream.

Cinnamon Apple Microwave Chips

Ingredients:

- 1 apple
- 1 tablespoon of cinnamon
- 1 tablespoon of granulated sugar

Instructions:

1. Slice the apple thinly and arrange the slices on a microwave-safe plate.
2. Sprinkle the cinnamon and sugar evenly over the apple slices.
3. Microwave on high for 3-5 minutes, or until the apple chips are crispy and lightly browned.
4. Let cool for a few minutes before serving.
5. Enjoy as a sweet snack or use as a topping for oatmeal or yogurt.